Dear Rhonda

Villard 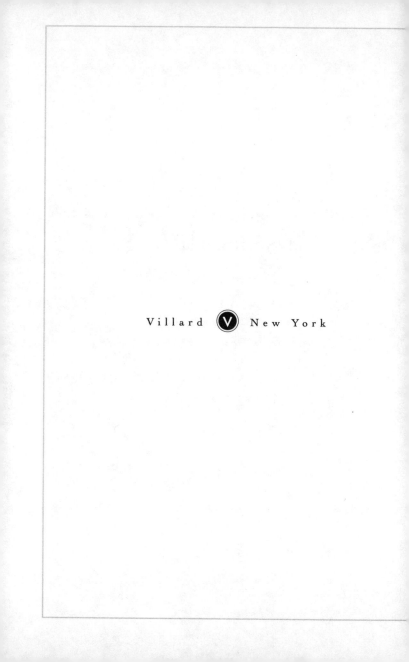 New York

Dear Rhonda

LIFE LESSONS
FROM A FATHER
TO HIS DAUGHTER

Demitri Kornegay

All rights reserved under International and Pan-American
Copyright Conventions. Published in the United States by
Villard Books, a division of Random House, Inc., New York,
and simultaneously in Canada by Random House of
Canada Limited, Toronto.

VILLARD BOOKS is a registered trademark of
Random House, Inc.
Colophon is a trademark of Random House, Inc.

ISBN 0-375-50842-2

Villard Books website address: www.villard.com
Printed in the United States of America on acid-free paper

2   4   6   8   9   7   5   3

First Edition

Book design by Deborah Kerner/Dancing Bears Design

To Rhonda, Tracy,
Jean, Chanel,
Brandi, Jazman,
Courtney, Erica,
Tiffany, Tasha,
Rhashad, Lovette,
Danielle, Zamira,
and any other young woman
who's wondering . . .

Acknowledgments

I have always felt it was my life's mission to do the best I possibly could with whatever tools I had. I must, then, first thank God for allowing me to cross paths with the right people at the right time, so that even if I didn't do it, at least I knew what was the right thing to do at the time.

To my wife, Angela, who has always been a loving source of support and encouragement. To my daughter, Rhonda, the original reason this book was written. To my parents, Elisha and Emma Kornegay, for providing an atmosphere of love and safety for their children that was totally conducive to education that would not tolerate "average" work.

To my maternal and paternal grandparents, all from Jones County, North Carolina; although my time with them was too brief, they still managed to teach me some of their "country common sense." To my brothers and sisters, who taught me to share. To my best friends, for being excellent sounding boards. To my coworkers and church family, for teaching me patience.

To every uncle, coach, and pastor I've ever had, for teaching me how to coach, captain, lead, and play the game of life.

To Melody Guy, the "Velvet Whip," my editor and new favorite task mistress, whose drive and consistent support brought this project to Villard/Random House. To David Hale Smith, for coming in to save the day.

To John 3:16 Bookstore in Lanham, Maryland; Dar Es Salaam Bookstore in Riverdale, Maryland; and every bookstore owner who was willing to take a chance on a good idea.

To every high school student in the Washington metropolitan area I've ever had the good fortune to meet.

Contents

To Whom It May Concern

My reasons for writing these letters, which became the book you now hold, are twofold. First, I am a police officer. Because of the nature of my profession, there exists a high probability I may be killed in the line of duty. Knowing this, and acknowledging the fact that I have a daughter who has a right to expect her father to protect her from things that go bump in the night, to provide her with a three-dimensional example of how a man is supposed to talk, treat women, and support his family, and to prepare her for the world that awaits her, I felt it necessary to write her letters she could keep for always to use as a reference should I die before she has occasion to ask. I wrote these letters to Rhonda over the course of five years. Although Rhonda's mother and I divorced, I tried to remain a significant influence in Rhonda's life; I called her every day and never missed a first day of school (until she asked me to). With these letters, she will always know how I felt, what I said, what I thought she should do, and how to tackle a problem. With these letters, she should know I loved her enough to sacrifice my wants for her needs, enough to make the unpopular decisions that would make her dislike me for a little while but thank me later, enough to be the father more men should be.

Second, over the course of time, I came to realize there were more than a few young ladies who, for one reason or another, did not have a man around to protect them, provide for them, and prepare them for life. Why not share with them the same information? There wasn't a reason not to, and I really feel these letters to my daughter will help those young ladies and some older ladies too. So, without an excuse, here they are.

Just call me Dad or Uncle Metree or the big brother who won't let anybody pick on you. Your new nickname is Rhonda.

Dear Rhonda

18 Things to Remember

1. You ARE special.
2. God has an important job for you and everything you go through prepares you for it.
3. Everything will be all right in the morning; maybe not tomorrow morning, but one morning is going to come and everything will be all right.
4. Death is a fact of life.
5. Your work is your signature, what you leave to the world. Always do your best.
6. Everyone has an off day. This, too, shall pass.
7. Your reputation may precede you; make that a good thing.
8. You make your own luck by the amount of effort you bring to the table.
9. Everybody has an agenda.
10. Bad people do exist; be careful.
11. Romance is like a traffic accident: the slower you go, the less damage you do.

12. All you have to do is breathe and some people won't like you, will be jealous of you, and will talk about you. Ignore them.

13. If your intentions are pure, unselfish, and good, God will bring them to life.

14. If your actions are evil, self-centered, and mean, God will bring you to task.

15. You ARE the star of this epic production called your life. Everyone chooses their own director. Some are directed by greed, lust, boyfriends, girlfriends, husbands, wives, status, loneliness, or vengeance. I recommend choosing God as your director.

16. Love can make fools or geniuses of us all.

17. Don't be impatient; be efficient with your time.

18. Every new morning you see is God's way of saying, "Get up and go try it again."

Adjusting to New Things

Dear Rhonda,

Enclosed is a newspaper article concerning ninth graders in the D.C. metropolitan area and how difficult it has been for them to adjust to their first year of high school. Problems ranged from being overwhelmed by the size of the school to being afraid to ask what might be considered a "stupid" question. A few of the students said they had problems making new friends and didn't know how to use their planners or study for all the different classes.

After reading the article, it occurred to me that these problems don't sound so different from the complaints college freshmen make when they are away from home for the first time.

The main difference would be that in high school, if students don't do well, they have to repeat ninth grade, but in college, if you don't do well, first you are put on academic probation and then you flunk out, never to return. There are scores of people who use the excuse, "Well, college just wasn't for me," when they know in their hearts they just didn't try hard enough.

They got to school and, drunk with their new-found freedom, realized they could stay up and stay out as long as they pleased. They could go to class when and if they felt like it, and their teachers wouldn't give them the blues about it. They ate when they wanted, they slept when they wanted, and before they knew it, they failed—which is what they didn't want.

Before you fix your mouth to give me that "Well, I just can't get it" business, let's remember you know the latest fashions, you've memorized all the words to the latest songs, and you've managed to stay on the honor roll.

What I'm saying is, you can get it if you stick with it. It's all about the level of importance you give things. You must understand—you have to learn all you can while you can. One of the hardest things to do is go back and learn a second or third time what you should have learned the first time. Many who say they'll put school on the back burner and come back later to get their education often don't go back for it at all.

Some quit college for what appears to be big bucks, only to discover they could have gone further if they'd stuck it out and earned their degree. They reach a certain level, then find they must go back to school to earn the degree they thought they'd be happy without. They watch as people who aren't as experienced go further because they have a degree.

It is written, "From whom much is given, much is required." Everything your mother and Angie and I and your uncles and aunts do for you is our way of investing in your potential.

At the age of 14 you've already done more than most Americans have. You've dined in stadium sky-boxes while watching professional sports contests. You've been to Disney World more times than I can remember, never missed a meal because of poverty, and have always gotten everything you wanted for Christmas. Now you're preparing to go to London, Paris, and Madrid for your spring break.

We do these things for you just as our parents did these things for us. We gave these things to you because we love you and expect the best for and from you. Now you have to love yourself enough to demand the best for and from yourself.

Girls who have not had the opportunities you've had are sometimes so easily impressed by the provider of those opportunities that they find themselves being forced to show their gratitude in ways that cost them their dignity and self-respect. We give you what we give you because we love you. Your smile and thank-you are gratitude enough. Some boys will try to impress you with things in order to make you feel you owe them something. Boys shouldn't be able to impress you with things you've already had. More on that later.

In your life you will have what are known as "the lean years." I never knew what a hungry day was until I was responsible for taking care of myself. Then there were plenty of hungry days, but I learned from them. I learned that although I was hungry, I wouldn't starve to death. I learned I could work and, if I handled my money wisely, put a roof over my head, clothes on my back, and food on my table without breaking the law or disrespecting myself. I learned to put my faith in God and my shoulder to the wheel. I learned a task is only hard work if you don't want to do it, and I learned if I managed my time wisely in college, I could get A's in just about all my classes. I also learned it was possible for my classmates to have a party, a dance, or a serious throwdown jam without my being in attendance.

This brings us back full circle to school and what those ninth graders/college freshmen must come to realize.

1. Everyone is new at something at least once. If they're not, they've been where they are too long.

2. Things appear big the first few times you see them until you find your way around. Remember how large Hillcrest Heights Elementary School looked when you were in kindergarten? If you don't want to ask how to get somewhere, get a map. If they don't have one, be the first to make one.

3. If you want to make a friend, be a friend, but not too much too soon. Trust, love, and respect are things that must be earned.

4. When you study, leave no stone unturned so that when you put your pen down after taking the exam, you'll know in your heart you've done all you could to get an A. God and you are the only ones who will know whether or not you're lying.

There you have it, beautiful girlfriend. Instructions on how to get through not only high school but college too. You can do it. I know you can. If I can, you can, because you're much smarter than I (in some things).

There's nothing standing between you and the honor roll except air and opportunity. As far as I can see, you have plenty of both!

Love,
Dad

Beautiful Ugly People

Hello Rhonda,

While I'm here at work, I am thinking about you and some things you should know. For some reason it occurs to me that you should know about ugly beautiful people and beautiful ugly people.

You will meet some people in your life who may not be physically attractive or pleasing to the eye, but who are wonderful on the inside. Along the same line, you will meet some people who, although they look good and dress nicely and seem to say all the things you think you want to hear, have a personality with the ugliest face this side of a lemon-eating contest. You can perfume fertilizer and put it in a nice, pretty box, but it's still cow manure just the same. Far too many times people confuse good looks with good people.

If someone is truly good, it will radiate from the inside and show on the outside because, after all, it's what's inside that's important. Here's how to be a beautiful person:

When you are polite without being subservient (look it up) and considerate without being condescending (look it up). When you are kind without coddling. When you can diplomatically excuse yourself from the presence of fools. When you can realize that although there may be some good in everyone, it's up to you to decide how long you should wait for someone to show the good that may or may not be within.

When you are intelligent enough to realize that someone or something may not be in your best interest and that you can care without it costing you your self-esteem. You must do right, even when it would be easier to go along with the crowd doing wrong.

When you are smart enough to speak up for those who can't speak for themselves, without getting so caught up in the sound of your own voice you lose sight of the point and become the very thing you're speaking against.

When you can be a friend without being foolish by showing more gratitude than attitude, and when you can show love (First Corinthians, Chapter 13, tells what love is; substitute "love" for "charity") and realize love is being shown to you.

When you get to know God so well that you figure out Jesus did not come to earth to save the "perfect" people, just people like you and me. When you can learn all these things (and believe me, it takes a lifetime) and know enough to say you don't know enough, then you have become what the essence of true beauty is all about.

Before you say a word to anyone about anything, know that what you say should always go through three gates: The first gate—is it kind? (You'd be surprised how far a kind word will go.) The second gate—is it true? (Don't lie.) The third gate—is it necessary? (Does what you have to say need to be said?) Sometimes it's hard to get through all three, but in a lot of cases, two gates out of three isn't bad. As your great-grandfather, Floyd Odell Murphy Sr., used to say, "Never pass up an opportunity to keep your mouth shut."

Let us now examine the traits of the ugly beautiful people, the people we are talking about when the adjectives *selfish, greedy, mean, thieving, lying, slandering,* and *cheating* come to mind.

Some people are popular solely because they are good-looking. Good looks can be lost in an instant (car accident, etc.), and if that's all you had, you won't be popular for long. You can wear a beautiful dress, but an ugly attitude will make you slouch. You can sport a pretty hairdo, but an ugly thought will make you frown.

I know you've heard it said at least once: "It's not enough for you to be in church; the question is whether or not the church is in you." Speaking of church, isn't it funny how some people are so good at speaking in tongues in church, but out of church they think they're too good to speak to you?

Ugly beautiful people all seem to share one common trait, despite the fact they come in all different shapes, colors, and sizes: They think they are better than anyone else. Although some people do some things better than others, no one is any better than anyone else.

Someone once said, "Beauty is in the eye of the beholder." Now, that's true. You're always going to have those friends who will see something beautiful in someone or something that you can't see. The musical group Tower of Power once sang a song that asked the question "What Is Hip?" One line in the song says, "If it's really hip, the passing years will show."

True beauty is the same way. If someone is really beautiful, the memories of their words and deeds will reveal their beauty down through the ages. In other words, in order to be *truly* beautiful, you do beautiful things for the right reason.

Love Always,
Daddy

Race Relations and Money

Rhonda,

A recent newspaper article told about a march for freedom that was conducted some 31 years ago from Selma, Alabama, to Montgomery, Alabama. As hard as it may be to believe, as late as 1965 there were white people in this country who honestly believed African Americans (we were called "colored" or "Negroes" then) should not have the right to vote for their governing officials.

There was no BET (Black Entertainment Television); in fact, you could watch television and rarely see a single black face. Schools were segregated, or separated by race, then also. Black people went to one school and white people went to another. Somehow (I'm sure it was all quite by accident) the good, new, up-to-date stuff went to the schools white children attended, while the old, outdated items wound up at the schools black children went to.

Poor facilities, poor equipment, outdated books, and teachers who spent more time keeping the class in order than teaching all led to poor education or no education for students, which, in turn, meant they couldn't compete with those students who had better facilities and newer books. These students weren't eligible for the better jobs because they lacked the fundamentals that would allow them to qualify. The better jobs pay more. If you are paid more, you should be able to live better and live where you want.

That was covered, too, by a system the banks, real estate agents, and insurance companies used called "redlining." You see, whenever a black person had enough money to live wherever he wanted to, but attempted to borrow money from a bank or get insurance for his car or find a home in a nice neighborhood, the bank would find a reason to say no, the insurance would be too high, and the real estate agent would take the black client to a neighborhood only black people lived in. A red line would surround black neighborhoods on a map or be drawn through a black person's name, and the black people wouldn't be able to get the same things white people with less money could. It still goes on today; it's just hidden better and laws are in place that are sometimes enforced against redlining.

Unfortunately, some persons of color believe that if they make more money, they'll automatically be treated fairly. Some even believe that the better they entertain, the more money and preferential treatment they'll receive. To an extent, that is true. If someone does something better than anyone else, they usually are paid more. The problem is, if they do what they do solely for the money and the influence they believe it will bring, money becomes the only love. Money is not the root of all evil; the *love* of money (greed) is the root of all evil.

If you are well paid, you should be living well. It's all about whether you spend your money or your money spends you. A fool with a million dollars won't be a millionaire very long; that fool will find himself with plenty of friends who, of course, have marvelous suggestions on how that million dollars should be spent (for examples, look up boxers, basketball players, and singers). From time to time you've heard me play a song by a singer named Bobby Womack called, "Nobody Wants You When You're Down and Out." Listen to it the next time you get a chance.

Some people get money and get "new." Suddenly they become "all that" because they drive certain types of cars. (All a car is supposed to do is get you from point A to point B, anyway.) They feel they've "arrived" because they wear DKNY T-shirts or Tommy Hilfiger outfits or Eddie Bauer coats or Timberland boots or Nautica jackets. I don't know why, but I've always had a problem with wearing someone else's name on my butt, back, chest, or feet when the name *Kornegay* or the person in those clothes should be what's most important. Certain names and brands are known for quality, but every morning you have an opportunity to be known as a person of quality, regardless of your attire. It's taking the people in this country too long to realize quality comes in all colors.

People of quality and who are qualified know God, are realistic, take pride in their work, stretch for their goals, remember the proper rules to live by, and attain the things they want in life legitimately. They don't get "new" when they hit it big. They remember where they came from, treat people like they'd want to be treated, and always try to do what they say they're going to do.

I'm sure you're acquainted with the term *wolf in sheep's clothing.* Well, nowadays it's not popular to say things like, "We don't want black people in our schools or neighborhoods, or in certain jobs or positions." Instead of saying that, they now say, "We only want 'qualified' people." How do you get to be qualified? Education. Opportunity. Things some African Americans may not have equal access to.

18

By now you should know information is power, and the more information you have, the more personal power you attain. So why is it all you'll find in the schools in the poor neighborhoods are the best-dressed attendees? Because a lot of their self-worth is wrapped up in the clothes they wear. They may not have it, but they want to look like they do. Now I didn't say "students" because attendees aren't students. They just hang out in the streets and schools or around the students.

One popular theory was that if black people sat in the decision-making positions on school boards and city councils, predominantly black schools would improve. They have not and even in this there is a lesson to be learned. Although they say they are fighting to ensure the people they represent receive an education that is just as good as what the well-to-do get, they are sometimes just as sorry and make decisions that are just as bad as the people who were there before, and that we should remember. This is what happens when you place your ethics, values, or principles up for sale to the highest bidder. (Remember what I told you about getting "new" when you get to a certain level you hadn't been to before.)

There are those black people who will say, "Vote

for me because I'm black." That's just as bad as saying, "A vote for me keeps a black man out." Honesty, justice, and fairness don't have a color. Every white man is not your enemy and every black man is not your friend.

Don't get me wrong; people coming out of the worst circumstances manage to excel and prosper. It's just harder. To move up to the next level you must be qualified. Go get qualified and don't ever forget what some people had to go through so you would get half a chance.

Why does the word *hood* have such a negative connotation? By not keeping our neighborhoods clean, not getting the proper education, and using illegal drugs, we are saying to those people who were beaten by policemen, chewed by dogs, burned out of their homes, and bombed out of their churches: You marched for nothing. We must stop allowing those persons who are too lazy to work, be parents, or who just don't know to use the neighborhood or schools or politicians as an excuse for the way they live. Ignorance is not a culture.

Let's use geometry and the "if/then" equation. If you want better neighborhoods, then start by cleaning them up, getting to know your neighbors, and fostering pride in where you live. If you want better schools for the children, then start attending PTA and school board meetings and holding the folks who sit on those councils accountable for what they do. If you want to get the illegal drugs out of your neighborhood, then inform the drug dealer, who probably lives in the neighborhood, he should leave because the police are coming, there's a job fair Monday morning at the employment office, and the councilperson who represents this area is going to be forced to camp out here until the illegal drug activity ceases.

Life is NOT a rap video. Times were much harder for your grandparents than anyone who has ever done a rap video could ever imagine, and your grandparents didn't resort to crime.

All that's really needed to be a success in life is inspiration, initiative, and imagination. If you've got at least one of those qualities, God will get you the other two.

I'm proud of you. Go make me prouder.

Love,
Dad

How to Change the World

Rhonda,

Enclosed is an interesting news article about Hamilton Earl Holmes, the first black man ever to be admitted to and attend classes at the University of Georgia. Although you may never find his name in any of the history books, he is a man who made history instead of waiting for someone else to come along and do it.

In these times of people complaining about the federal government intruding into their lives, saying the state should decide what happens in their own local areas, we must remember not long ago black people were not allowed into universities, neighborhoods, hospitals, or restaurants, or allowed to have good jobs, for no other reason than because they were black. It was only when the federal government intervened, or came in to settle the matter, that local and state governments begrudgingly (slowly, with complaints) began to treat blacks fairly. These things can be easily forgotten if we allow them to be.

Jewish people will never let anyone forget how

many of their people were murdered in the death camps during World War II. After the war, they worked, set up an economic base by opening and running their own legitimate businesses, and then became a political force to be reckoned with in this country. Black people must never forget the mistreatment our elders had to endure and the mistreatment others still undergo for no reason other than the fact that we are black.

In this society, some people feel that because you are black and they are not, they are better than you. There are even black people who will mistreat, abuse, rob, and murder another black person before they would harm anyone else because they don't think much of themselves and know the criminal justice system has historically given harsher penalties to blacks who hurt whites than to blacks who hurt blacks. Department of Justice statistics have shown it is a fact that black people who commit the same crime as white people go to jail more often and stay there longer than the white offenders.

Don't get me wrong; I don't care who you are, if you commit a crime, I believe you should go to jail AND pay reparations to the victim, but it isn't fair for the rich to walk away from a crime the poor have to stay and pay for. It's a fact that most rich criminals are white and most poor criminals are black.

We must, like many other people of different ethnic origins, set up our own economic base, and opening and running our own legitimate businesses are just a start in that direction. By becoming organized, we can recognize our responsibilities and then make ourselves a political force to be reckoned with. Not by dividing ourselves light against dark (we're all still black) or disliking someone because they live in Southeast or Fort Washington and we live in Silver Spring or Temple Hills, and not by committing crimes or doing anything "to survive" or "go for mine." That's a fool's way of doing things. First, because more often than not these idiots who commit crimes are hurting their own people when they shouldn't be hurting anyone, and second, because the people with all the money are building jails to put those idiots away and out of sight.

The way to bring about real positive change is not to jump up and down and hoop and holler or riot and burn. Jumping around is just an aerobic workout that will leave you tired, and the rioting and burning will not exactly benefit the neighborhoods of those persons who are upset. Somehow the logic of burning down my own house, grocery store, or pharmacy be-cause I'm mad at people who live far away doesn't make sense. Yet it happens because some people are so angry they don't know how to control their rage.

Avoid these people at all costs. They will only hurt themselves and you.

The way to bring about change that will last is to work your way up within your chosen system, the way your mother and I have. It's not a perfect system, but it's the best one in the world, and because we live here, it's the only one we have.

We must improve ourselves mentally. We must improve our thought processes and our thinking in general. Everyone loves Michael Jordan and all those other black entertainers, but I'm willing to bet the people who pay them are billionaires who probably never set foot on a stage, football field, or baseball di-amond. They don't break a sweat, yet they make all the money.

I suppose what I'm saying is, I would rather be the one who pays Michael Jordan than be Michael Jordan, because the one who does the paying is the boss. The one who is paid is the employee. Be a boss. Learn how to be a boss, then go be one. That takes mental strength. Exercise your mind.

Focus on power. Power is the ability to define your own reality and exercise control over it. You may not start out with what you think is a lot, but consider this: You have your health and the ability to choose which way your life will go. Everyone has the power of choice. Some are afraid to make the necessary choices and will attempt to disguise their fear with loud talk and wrong action. No matter what excuse they give, they and you still have a choice. God has given it to us, and what God gives us no one can take away—*we give it away*. But even if you give it away, you can always take it back.

Anyone who stands in the way of your reaching your fullest spiritual, mental, and physical potential should be fired.

Hamilton Earl Holmes lived up to his mental potential. Read how he did it and what he had to go through so you and I could live better lives.

Love,
Dad

Depression

Dear Rhonda,

When I called you on the phone, you sounded so sad and you tried to make me believe nothing was wrong. Please try to remember, it's my job to tell when things are wrong and make them right, and more important, as your father it's my job to help you through these things.

After I asked you a few more times what was wrong, you finally confessed you were depressed. Being depressed is not a unique thing. Sooner or later in life, everyone gets depressed. What's truly important is how you handle your depression. Do you overtake it or do you allow it to overtake you? No one is happy all the time or depressed all the time; if they seem to be, they need counseling.

New York State's Commission on Quality of Care recently published a series of articles regarding clinical depression and major depressive disorders. The articles were written by high schoolers, people in your age group, some of whom felt withdrawn from society, sadness without cause, hopelessness, and unfounded guilt. Quite a few of these young persons were preoccupied with death and suicide. These are the symptoms of clinical depression. Should you or anyone you know start and sustain these feelings for more than two weeks, counseling from a psychiatrist, psychologist, social worker, or trusted friend is definitely in order. Make sure you or they follow up with some form of professional help.

You are at what is known as an awkward age — adolescence. You feel like a grown-up whom everyone treats like a kid, but you're really a kid everyone expects to act like a grown-up. When someone tells you to do something, you become angry because you feel they shouldn't have to tell you what to do. You're angry at yourself for not figuring it out first so they wouldn't have to tell you. You're angry at them. You're angry at every little thing. Don't worry, everyone older than 25 has gone through this. Some come out of it better than others.

Here are some positive ways to get through the angry period: (1) try to think of something funny that, in the past, made you laugh uncontrollably; (2) go to your room and pray that whatever made you angry will go far, far away but not before the bluebird of happiness gets over a bout of constipation on their shoulder; (3) keep repeating to yourself, "this too shall pass"; (4) count to 235; (5) sit down and honestly think about what life would be like if that person who made you angry or depressed wasn't around anymore and wasn't ever coming back.

Now, let's discuss depression. It's just a pity party the devil talks you into throwing yourself. I know some things will occur in your life that will make you sad, and it's all right to cry. Just remember some folks will do some really rotten things to you, just so they can see your reaction. I say, don't give them the satisfaction of knowing they upset you. Living well is the best revenge.

When I begin to become depressed, I feel it's the best time to take inventory of some of the blessings the Lord has given me. I can see, and a lot of people who can't would love to be able to. I can hear, and a lot of people who can't would love to be able to. I can walk, and even run, and I know a lot of people would give anything to be able to move their arms and legs. Oh, to be able to climb a flight of stairs or run errands for their mother!

We sometimes take for granted the things we do every day until we can't do them anymore. It's the same way with people: We are sometimes lulled into a false sense of "they'll always be there," until they die or move away. Then we are consumed with what we should have done while they were here. That's why I try to let everyone who is dear to me know it every time I see them, even if I am angry with them. I was once told to treat everyone I love as if they were going to die tomorrow, because one day, I'll be right.

When your grandmother died, I was very angry and depressed and I cried a lot. I still do sometimes, but rather than focus on my depression, I've decided to help other people who need assistance. That way I stop focusing so much on myself and help someone who needs help. For instance, the Christmas after Grandma Emma died, I bought a whole boatload of stuffed animals for the children who were sick in the hospital. I think they felt better and I did too. What I'm saying is, if you stop concentrating on what's wrong and start thinking about things YOU can make right, everyone wins.

Your solution doesn't have to be as expensive as stuffed animals. It could be something as simple as a card to someone you don't know on the "sick and shut-in" list at church or a "hello, how are you doing?" call to a relative who hasn't heard from you in a while.

You told me you didn't think anyone cared about you. Nothing could be further from the truth. Why, just today someone asked about you and inquired as to how you were doing. Just the smile you gave, your cheerful attitude, and the help you offered made those good people think of you in a favorable manner.

What's that you say? The "right" people don't care? How many times do I have to tell you that you can't make everyone like you? Some folks won't, just because, and that's their loss because they won't ever know the splendor and wonder of knowing what a simply marvelous individual you truly are. All that and a child of God. What's not to like? I'll say it again: Living well is the best revenge.

Don't ever become impatient; be efficient with your time. While you're waiting for whatever to come through, there's always something about yourself you could be improving, even if you are wonderful. Feel better now? Good!

Please don't ever lose the letters I've sent you. They'll make it easier for you as time goes by and when I'm not around.

Love,
Dad

Looking Ahead

Dear Rhonda,

Congratulations again on your graduation! In the future, the work will be harder, but the rewards will be even greater. As I looked at you and your fellow graduates, I was filled with anxious moments and earnest prayer that God would keep those evil predators who make up part of our "free" society away from them and you.

I prayed, For God's sake, let them be kids and have fun for at least a little while. Let them learn from their mistakes, but not too harshly. Let them have fun, but remember their purpose. When their hearts are broken, let their weeping endure for only a night. Let them gain experience from their losses and humility from their victories. Please help them understand that with every worthwhile endeavor there is struggle. Nothing of value is ever gained without it. Have them learn that struggle forms unbreakable bonds, it reveals one's true character (you never know what you'll do until you're put under pressure), and it gives one a greater sense of respect for the accomplishments of others.

I've been a police officer for 15 years now, and I've seen just about every kind of atrocity a human being could impose upon another person, place, or thing. I also believe most intelligent people can avoid becoming victims by simply refusing to place themselves in harm's way. This means being aware of everyone and everything around you. Your peripheral vision must work overtime.

Realize that anyone has the potential to do anything, if the proper circumstances exist. Trust Mom and Angie and Dad and a few other family members, but verify everything anybody else tries to tell you.

Remember the three things someone will use to take advantage of you: (1) sympathy—the quickest way to a woman's heart is through pity; (2) flattery— "ohh baby, you so fine!" and (3) ingenuine kindness— "I did this for you, you can't do that for me?" Anyone who does something for you with the expressed purpose of getting something in return is to be watched like a snake. They'll kill off all the little problems like mice and make it appear as though they're doing you a favor, while at any moment they may turn and strike you.

Use your head! If something is telling you it's time to leave and you're in a place you had questions about at the outset, get out! The worldly would call it survival instinct. The devout would suggest it's your guardian angel doing his or her job. The military would say it's time to readjust your position on the terrain. No matter how you choose to say it, do like they did in Amityville and get out.

I have enclosed a local newspaper put together by the various law enforcement agencies in the Washington metropolitan area. It comes complete with pictures of bad guys. If you look at each picture closely, you'll come to realize how some of the suspects in the paper look like people you'll see on the street, and how some of the people you see in the street look like they should be in that paper. What I'm saying is, be careful!

I've written hundreds of incident reports, from rapes to burglaries to con jobs, and the victims all have one thing in common: They never thought it would happen to them!

Sun Tzu, a Chinese general who was renowned for his cunning and strategic wisdom, once said, "The best way to avoid a war is to always be prepared for one." Remember that.

Don't be afraid, for God did not give us the spirit

of fear. Fear clouds the mind. Be careful. God *did* give us the power to choose. Everyone has a choice. You have been taught that choices are long-lasting and life-changing.

Don't become angry waiting for what you want; instead spend your time working on your own shortcomings or addressing a new challenge, like learning another language. Do all you can to make your own reality, and when you have, don't sit waiting and whining. Work on you. Surely there's something about your marvelous self you could be improving!

Don't ever forget that someone, somewhere, could earnestly use your help, and no matter how bad things seem, they can always be worse.

Don't take it for granted that you can see. Imagine life without sight. You can hear. Imagine life without sound. You can move. Imagine life without motion. Be thankful you have these abilities and use them to leave the world a better place than the way you found it.

I'm so proud of you and I know I'll be proud again.

Love,
Dad

Work

Rhonda,

Let's focus on work for a few minutes and what it can teach us. We can learn a lot from life and from the people and things around us if our eyes are open and we're willing to be taught.

I don't believe I've ever told you about the summer I worked at a construction site on the campus of the University of Richmond. Your uncle Kenny and I were attending summer school in college. The year was 1977 and we were staying in the barracks in the basement of the Robins Center (the basketball arena). We stayed in a room full of about 20 bunk beds but there were only about five or six of us.

Since there were no closets or dressers, everyone had his own little private area where he would either hang up his belongings on the edge of a bunk or lay them out across a nearby mattress. The room had only one two-plug electrical outlet, so we plugged a small portable refrigerator into one and an extension cord for the hot plate, stereo, toaster oven, television, and iron into the other. Before you say it, I understand now that it was dangerous and foolish.

Obviously, this was the summer I learned to "make do." In other words, I took a group of bunk beds and made them do the work of a closet and bureau. We took one bathroom equipped with one shower and made it do the work of seeing to the personal and hygienic needs of six young men. We took our initiative and drive to succeed and made it show us we had what it took to do whatever we wanted.

A typical day started with my rising at 5 A.M. to go on a five-mile run (we had to stay in shape for football). It would still be dark and everyone else would still be asleep, so I learned how to dress in my workout clothes in the dark. Upon my return at 6 A.M., the rest of the fellas knew it was time to get up and go to their construction jobs. The pay was good, but the work was dirty and hard: Regular construction hours are from 7 A.M. to 3 P.M. For me, it was a shower and breakfast (Frosted Flakes and milk are easiest to fix and store), clean up my area, and off to my eight o'clock class. Did I forget to mention your alarm clock becomes your best friend?

Classes were over at 10:30 A.M. I ate lunch on

my way to Channel 6. You see, I would go there for about an hour every day, Monday through Friday from 11 A.M. to noon, to learn television. I had made a deal with Mr. Shand, the station manager, that if he could get four of his employees to take 15 minutes out of their lunch hour to show me what they knew about television, someday I'd be able to run his station all by myself. Of course, he thought I was bragging or joking, so he arranged it just to prove me wrong. I don't believe he thought I'd keep coming back every day — but I did and I made a point of trying to learn something every day. Channel 6 did not have an internship program at the time.

I had already been an intern with the late Ron Sutton at WHUR radio in Washington, D.C., the summer before. That's right, your old man once worked at WHUR. It was the end of my freshman year, and I wanted to major in communications so I just went around and asked about internships.

People don't like to hire you unless you have experience; how do you get experience if they won't hire you? You volunteer, you offer your services in exchange for knowledge, you apply for an internship — you do something! Managers don't like to take chances on anyone, but they're more likely to take a chance on a young person who is inexperienced and therefore doesn't cost as much to pay. When you're young, don't worry about how much you're not getting paid in money. Focus instead on what knowledge and skills you can gain.

After spending just an hour at Channel 6, I went back out to campus where I was employed as a part-time helper at the new science center's construction site. I swept up the dust, handed electricians wires and plumbers pipes, and worked with people I won't say made bad decisions, just decisions I didn't have to or wouldn't want to make.

Some of the guys I worked with were only 16 or 17, yet they were already married with two or three children. When I asked them how they could do that (I was 19 at the time), they told me they'd gotten their girlfriends pregnant and were only doing the right thing. Here I was, working for spending money so your grandmother wouldn't have to send me any, and these guys were making the little bit they were getting stretch to feed and clothe an entire family.

To top it off, we had an absolute, dyed-in-the-wool, rednecked bigot for a foreman, one who didn't like blacks because they were black, who didn't like the young white guys and called them trash, and who hated me because I was in college. At first he tried the old divide-and-conquer routine. Whenever I arrived at the work site, he would announce to the other workers, "The college boy is stopping by to pick up a check. Hey professor, you learn a new way to put these boys out of a job? Hey, Mr. Fancy Proper-talk, ah'm talkie' to you, boy!" I'd ignore him and they'd ignore me. It went on that way until one day one of the guys was trying to fill out a job application during break. I offered to help and he was so desperate he accepted my aid. If he had said no then that wouldn't have been a big deal either.

Seeing me help that guy broke the ice and showed the other guys I wasn't the stuck-up person the foreman told them I was. From that point on, we talked, exchanged views, discussed life, and shared plans for our futures. The guy I helped got the job. There was hope on the construction workers' faces and disgust on the foreman's. I knew that meant soon (and very soon), one way or another, I was going to have to go.

Despite his attempts to bait me into a fight, I simply outthought the foreman. Some people's minds are so clouded with hate and ignorance that they can't think straight. That is why I tell you he or she who loses control loses. The foreman needed us workers fighting one another. That is how he believed he maintained control. That way, he felt superior. If we stopped fighting and started looking at who was instigating the fight, he would be found out.

I had a goal: Earn money for school clothes so your grandmother, who was already sending money to your aunt Kaye and uncle Darryl, wouldn't have to send any to me. Plus, this was only part-time from 12:30 to 3 P.M. After I finished work, I'd shower, work out for about two hours, shower again, eat, and go to bed. That was my day. We often look back and wonder how we fit all those things in.

In the end, we knew it was because God had given us the wisdom to be efficient with our time instead of impatient, the knowledge to realize we were young and would have to pay our dues to be successful, and most important, the vision to see we weren't staying in this present predicament. We were going THROUGH.

It's always a lot easier when you realize this is just something you have to go through, like a tunnel. You don't come out the way you went in. You should come out of every incident in your life a little wiser. You may pick up a few scars, emotional and otherwise, but as long as you've learned something, it wasn't a waste of your time.

One day, the foreman wanted some of the portable rest rooms mopped, and he decided I was the only one who could do it. They had never been mopped before (and probably haven't since), but he didn't care. He was going to play with the "college boy's" head.

"First," he said, "I need the rest rooms mopped and then the Sani-Jons, so my workingmen can have a clean place to sh— —." Determined not to let him anger me and knowing your great-grandparents had endured worse than this, I was willing to mop the building rest rooms, but doing the disposable Sani-Jons was going to be a bit too much. I found out by accident (God lets us find out things on purpose that we think are by accident) that he had hidden the mop and bucket. Rather than get upset, I assisted the others until the foreman entered, looked me in the eye, and said, "Boy, didn't I tell you to clean out the sh— —holes so my men would have a clean place to sh— —?" He went on before I could answer. "Can't you follow instructions, college boy? I seen you carry all them books around, but you can't even find a mop and a bucket, much less know what to do with 'em.

Just another dumb nigger," he muttered, turning away from me.

I looked him right in the pupils and made him nervous when I spoke in a tone I didn't know I had. "Excuse me," I growled.

"What, boy?" he said, shaking from rage and fear.

"What did you say?"

"I said you can't even find—"

"'The mop and bucket from where you hid them." I finished his sentence.

"What the hell is this?" he screamed as he pulled the items from the rear of his pickup.

"It looks like the mop and bucket you hid before you asked me to clean the sh——holes so your men could have a clean place to sh——."

"Hid it?" he screamed.

"Yes," I said, calming myself. "In all this big construction site everyone here knows the cleaning utensils are kept in the storeroom over there." I pointed in the opposite direction. "You just took the mop and bucket out the back of your truck."

The truth had come to light, and everyone who hadn't already realized it did at that moment.

"Why, you uppity, smart-assed, nigg—"

"The next time you call me nigger you'll be getting up off the ground."

"You, you're fired!" he screamed. "Go up to Lucky's trailer and git your pay."

I looked around at the architecture and smiled.

"Didn't chew hear me?"

I walked to the men I had worked beside who had become my coworkers, shook their hands, and said in a loud voice without looking at the foreman, "I'll be going to school here in the fall and then I'll graduate with a good education, but you, you'll still be the same stupid racist bastard you are right now."

He started to come at me with the mop in his hands. Instead of running like I knew he expected, I broke down into the perfect linebacker's two-point stance and said, "Bring it." He stopped and yelled, "Get the hell off my site!" I told your grandmother about it that night. She asked, had I hit him at all? When I told her I hadn't, she sounded almost disappointed but said it was probably better I didn't.

The next week I got a job as a salesclerk in the Limited clothing store at Regency Square Mall. I spent most of my time polishing the chrome and mirrors, but the store was air-conditioned and the summer was practically over anyway. It was time for football practice.

The next summer Mr. Shand called me and said Channel 6 was starting an internship program and asked if I would be interested in being the South's First Television Station's first intern? You know I said yes. You know something else? Two years later I wound up running the television station all by myself on a Thanksgiving morning, like I said I would. Remember how I told you no experience is a waste of time as long as you manage to learn something from it? Well, as my experiences at the construction site that summer taught me, sometimes you should work at a job for a little while to see what you *don't* want to do for the rest of your life.

Love,
Dad

Dating

Dear Rhonda,

You're 15, you have the body of a grown woman, and you're thinking about boys, dating, love, and sex.

I'm 41, a grown man, and I had to be 15, 16, 17, 18, 19, and so on before I could get to 41, so I know what and how men think. You should know, too, so you can act responsibly.

Although the rules of courtship have been allowed to change over the years, the goals are still the same. For some girls, the goal is the love and adoration they feel they don't get at home. For some boys and men, the goal is how many girls they can have sex with so they can brag about it to their friends later. For some, it's also the ability to dominate and control another person, while others want nothing more than purely physical contact. Lastly, it's the attention from someone, anyone, that some people will do anything for.

Let's start with the dress code. A lot has been said about how this is America and everyone (meaning women) should be able to wear what they want without being accosted by cretins and lowlifes. Even Queen Latifah in her song "U.N.I.T.Y." talked about wearing "booty-cutter shorts 'cause it was crazy hot" and having someone approach her incorrectly. The good Queen remedied the problem by correcting the offender immediately. If she had not said anything, the offending party might have walked away from the situation with the idea that his conduct was acceptable. I don't know how many times I've heard, "Well, she didn't say anything," offered as an excuse for improper behavior. Some things need to be, as Barney Fife would say, "nipped in the bud."

You should be able to wear what you like, but think about what your attire says about you. Like the commercial says, you never get a second chance to make a first impression. The first thing most people see when they see you is what you have on and how you're wearing it.

Trends and fads come and go, but class and style are forever. There is a thing called "country common sense," and one of its rules is, it may not be new, but it can always be clean. Think clothing and residence when you think about this rule. If you wish to be seen as a classy person, you should dress and carry yourself with class. Class is nothing more than being kinder, more gracious, and more generous than others expect you to be.

There are those persons who dress provocatively, showing everything they have and then some. So what? This is still America. The problem is their freedom of expression through attire may be taken as an invitation by those members of our free society who were never taught to look but not touch. Know this and be prepared. I know I've said many times not to allow your fear of car thieves to determine what kind of car you will drive, your fear of burglars to determine what you'll put in your home, or someone else's opinion of you to define your reality, but your body is yours and there are too many men everywhere who won't take no for an answer.

Remember the movie *Face/Off*, when John Travolta told his daughter, "If you dress like Halloween, ghouls will try to get in your pants." Sometimes people do what they do as a plea for attention. We talked about the guys in their cars with the music playing at concert pitch. They're saying, "Hey, look at me. My music's louder than anyone's." (Scientists have discovered music played disgustingly loud over a continued period of time causes sterility and deafness in laboratory animals. In ten years, these guys won't be able to have children, and whispering sweet nothings in their ears will truly be pointless.)

Last winter, on a cold day, we rode past a girl about your age wearing some "Daisy Duke" shorts, and I pointed out to you that she was clearly screaming for attention. Is risking pneumonia or the attention of a potential sex offender worth it?

Even if the young lady is classy but dresses like she's in a 2 Live Crew video, if she does get a decent guy's attention, he'll do one of two things: (1) encourage and allow her to keep dressing like that because he likes to see other men lusting for what is "his" exclusively, or (2) try to change her dress code because he doesn't want the fellas seeing too much of what he's got.

One of the first rules of public speaking is to know your audience. Upon deciding what to wear when you venture outside your home, the same rule should apply.

The term *lover* has been replaced by *mack daddy* and *player*. Within my group of friends, we had a saying, "If it's a game, let EVERYBODY know you're just playing." That way, no one can throw the truth up in your face. All the aforementioned term meant was, let the ladies know you're not looking to get serious, that you don't want a steady girlfriend or significant other. Let's just have some fun. Then we'd give our definition of fun, and see if our dates could get with that. That was it, pure and simple, no room for mis-understanding.

It's obvious that these days those rules have been thrown out the window. You're going to run into guys who will lie, front (pretend they're the preferred detergent when they're really "brand x"), and work on your sympathy in an attempt to get what they want, then be gone with the dawn. You already know the three ways to take advantage of anyone: sympathy, flattery, and ingenuine kindness.

When dealing with matters of the heart, our imagination can be our best and worst friend. Case in point: I still have lofty dreams of Halle Berry, Lela Rochon, or any member of En Vogue telling Oprah and the nation what a wonderful man they've found in me.

Now, back to reality. Songs have been written about a love gone wrong ("Give Me the Reason," Luther Vandross), not having a love ("Any Love," Luther Vandross), a love that's growing ("Heaven Knows," Luther Vandross)—maybe somebody ought to talk to Luther—being in love with someone who's your best friend ("Save the Best for Last," Vanessa Williams), and being in love with someone who doesn't even know you ("Just My Imagination," The Temptations).

One way or another, some form of all of the above will happen to you. Don't panic. It's normal for every healthy, well-adjusted person to have a period of time they reflect on and wonder, "What the hell was I thinking?" Fact is, they weren't thinking and that's why what happened, happened.

Despite all the precautions, our hearts will be broken or we'll wind up breaking somebody else's heart. In either case, when this occurs the same rule applies: Always be a class act. If you're the one who is hurt, bow out gracefully, do not resort to violence, and get on with your life. You existed before you knew the guy who broke your heart, and, like the song says, you will survive. Whenever our hearts were broken my friends and I had a rule: Everything will be all right in the morning. We don't know what morning, but one morning's gonna come and everything will be all right.

You'll feel sad and it'll look like everybody's got somebody except you. You'll relate to sad records on the radio and cry, but remember, this is something

you're going through. The key word here is *through.*
You will be the one who decides when you check out
of Heartbreak Hotel. When you do, don't just rush
into another relationship.

People that rush into relationships all excited
about their newfound love often lose interest once the
newness wears off and they see what they've really got.
Just remember the reason relationships are like car
accidents—the slower you go, the less damage you do.

People who rush into relationships often look
only for the good stuff and are so optimistic they see a
mud slide as a wonderful way to turn over new soil.
The guy or girl could scratch private places in public,
call undue attention to their own flatulence (look it
up) while sitting at the dinner table with your super-
visor, wink at your pastor's wife during Easter Sunday service, or run into your house screaming, "When
the police get here, I was with you all day, okay?" and
the most their thoroughly smitten, starry-eyed love
interest would utter would be, "She/He is so color-
ful!" They overlook things. Horrible, horrible things.
Red flags go up. The robot from *Lost in Space* is
screaming, "DANGER, DANGER, WILL ROBIN-
SON!" But they're in love and it's okay—for now.

When it's new, it's "Oh, that will change." When it's not, it's "Why don't you change?" When it's over, it's "He wouldn't change."

Moral: Don't try to change people. Look at his worst habit, magnify it by ten, and honestly think about whether or not you can deal with it.

Some guys may change for the worse because for them, the pursuit is gone. They've got you. They may then want to see how much abuse you'll take. When they do, moonwalk with all deliberate speed out of the relationship. The Lord has somebody better in mind for you. You just met that chump so you'd know a good thing when you get it.

If you're the one doing the heartbreaking, do it gently and go away. Say something like, "Perhaps I'm not what you need right now. You have so much to offer, and frankly, I'm not prepared to fully appreciate it at this time." Let them down gently, even if they are jerks. (Remember, always be a class act!) They'll be missing you long after you've forgotten them.

Quietly avoid being in the same hemisphere with them if you can. Don't make a big deal out of it, but try to steer clear of the guy and his fragile ego for about a month or until he rebounds into another relationship. The last thing either of you needs is a constant reminder of something that went wrong.

Nobody, not even you, is perfect. You do, however, deserve the best—as long as you're trying to be the best. Always go for that.

Love,
Dad

Decisions

Dear Rhonda,

A few weeks ago, I told you about an article I read in the paper about a few teenage girls who have a responsibility thrust upon them because they made the wrong choice. You know how it is with choices: Some are so easy to make they are called "slam dunks" or "no-brainers," but it's the difficult choices we are forced to make that truly test us. There will be times you will find yourself in the position where you must make those difficult choices. Here are some helpful tips to get you through those really trying times.

First, decide if you really *have* to make a choice. You could be venturing haphazardly into an area you're not fully prepared for, and when that happens, or when you are rushed by another into making a decision, the results are usually disastrous. If you question your preparedness, consult an older, wiser individual who is not involved with the choice but who has your best potential in mind. (Hint: Why let someone offer to fix your car when theirs doesn't work?)

If you are being rushed into a decision by someone else, ask yourself, "Why is this person rushing me and what do they have to gain from MY decision?" Know this: EVERYONE has his or her own agenda, or set of plans. You can choose whether you wish to be a participant in that agenda or follow your own schedule.

As we get older and widen our circles of friends, many times we are called upon to make the dreaded "good bad" or "bad good" decisions. In other words, sometimes the decision we have to make may make us feel good for a little while but bad in the long run, and sometimes the decision we make causes us to feel bad for a little while, but we realize in the long run that it was a good choice.

Here's an example. As I told you in the previous letter, in most boyfriend-girlfriend relationships, everything usually goes along wonderfully when you first start out because you're both trying to impress each other with how wonderful you both are. Both of you are apt to overlook those things about each other you don't really care for. Even when one of you does something really wrong, the tendency for most of us is to overlook the offense because the newness of the relationship hasn't rubbed off yet.

It is during this period things that should not be allowed often are. Girlfriends are called "bitch," are expected to cover the costs of admission to movies and concerts and to lend out their cars, and should their newfound loves have a really bad day, take the occasional slap in the face.

Listen carefully: ABUSE IN ANY FORM IS NOT TO BE TOLERATED. I DON'T CARE IF HE LOOKS LIKE DENZEL WASHINGTON AND HAS A DONALD TRUMP WALLET!

No matter how many times he says he's sorry, no matter how "fine" he is, no matter how "phat" or popular, one abuse, physical or mental, and it's five, four, three, two, your time is up!

I have learned in relationships that if someone is in a rush to get things started, step back and allow them to rush on to the next person. There is always time for you to work on being the best *you* while you wait for the Lord to send you the right person. There are always more things for you to learn, more languages for you to try, more unselfish acts for you to commit while the Lord works on a suitable boyfriend for you. What I'm saying again is: Don't be impatient; be efficient with your time.

Some choices are easy to make in theory but

harder to make in real life. Would you sleep with a guy you know has AIDS? Of course not. Now, would you sleep with a guy who seems to be the man of your dreams, whom you haven't known long, but whom you have good feelings about? How do you know he doesn't have AIDS? The fact is, you don't.

Whenever you're faced with a dilemma and you really wonder whether you should or shouldn't do something or say something, ask yourself this: Would I do this or say this if my mother or father or Jesus was standing beside me watching?

Don't get caught up in a wave of emotion, no matter what type. It's easy to say, "I lost control." He or she who loses control loses. This is where self-discipline comes in. Self-discipline is no more than relying on ourselves to employ that same common sense we believe others lack.

The newspaper article enclosed is about girls, some your age, who had decisions to make.

They made the wrong choices. See how much harder they have made it for themselves? The younger you are when you have a child, the more apt you are to be poor the rest of your life.

In the article, you may notice not too much is said about the boys who helped them get pregnant.

That's because despite how much boys promise they'll love you forever and they'll always be there for you, the moment a girl gets pregnant, she goes from being "my lady," "my girl," "my woman," "my Boo," to "my baby's mother" or "my baby's muva." The baby's father isn't there because he's a player who's off to romance somebody new. Why change diapers when you can change phone numbers? They'll tell you you're ready for love, but examine the look on their faces when you ask if they're ready to be a father.

Here's a secret everyone knows but no one says out loud: Men/boys will lie through their teeth to get into your pants. Remember that. How do I know? Strange as it seems, I was once that age and so were my friends. We talked and acted the same way, until a girl's father asked me if I was the type of guy I would want my daughter to go out with. If not, why not? That conversation made me look past a hot moment of emotion and right into the eyes of responsibility. I'd advise you and your friends to do the same.

After you finish reading the article, call me and tell me what you think.

Love,
Dad

Love and Marriage

Dear Rhonda,

Hopefully, someday you will meet a man, decide that you love him, and choose to marry him. In the preceding sentence I have just said a mouthful.

You will note I said, "meet a man." Not a boy, player, mack daddy, or smoothie, but a man. What is a man? A man is a male who is honest. He is reliable as well as self-reliant, and he assumes responsibility (a big, important word here) not only for his actions but for the actions of those persons he is responsible for.

There are many who call themselves men because they have a deep voice and a penis.

You have friends and relatives who will be willing to settle for that. If that's all they've got, they don't have enough. There are too many wrong definitions about what a man is.

Movies would have us believe a "real man" can kick everybody's butt like Steven Seagal or Sylvester Stallone or Arnold Schwarzenegger or Wesley Snipes. All the aforementioned action heroes do one thing that all real men do — save you from a bad life!

You'll find he doesn't have to fly a jet plane or fire a submachine gun to do that.

As a matter of fact, confident women with functioning brains are finding they are quite capable of sponsoring, bankrolling, and ensuring for themselves a good life, thank-you-very-much.

Unfortunately, too many folks within the black community earnestly believe you're not a real man until you've been to jail. More often than not, a trip to jail has cost some males their manhood.

A large degree of juvenile delinquency, the disruption of our schools, and the breakdown of families can be traced back to the fact that the appropriate males either didn't know how to be men or refused to be men and take on the responsibility of rearing their children. They had the sex but couldn't handle the hassle of taking care of what they helped create. Like cowards, they turned and ran from their responsibility.

I believe the reason it takes a sperm from a male and an egg from a female to make a child is because God meant for BOTH parents to create AND raise the child.

As we have seen from our own lives, Mom and Dad may not have been able to get along, but they got along long enough to make the child, so they should get along when it comes to matters concerning the child. You do not have to live under the same roof to do that.

As a man, I realize the way I conduct myself within your sight and hearing will be the gauge you use to determine what you will look for in and come to expect from a man.

A male will never be a man until he can be honest with and about himself and his actions. If he's lying to himself and can't respect himself, why should he tell the truth or respect you?

A male will never be a man until he can legitimately feed, dress, and care for himself.

Sons have their mamas and/or daddies to feed and dress them and put a roof over their heads. As long as they are doing so, those sons will be Mama's or Daddy's little boys. They won't do the hard work because Mama or Daddy has always done it for them. Old habits die hard. It's hard for me to just stand back and let you find out the satisfaction you're supposed to get in accomplishing a difficult task, but that is precisely what a parent is supposed to do—allow you to gradually discover that you can take on the difficult tasks without my help. It'll make it that much easier when you have a family of your own.

In our society, with its norms and mores (customs and traditions), we expect the man of the house to do the hard work. In a relationship, a woman should never have to do the hard work unless the man is doing most of it.

A male will never be a man until he is willing to lead or follow. There should be a purpose to his life. He should be willing to prepare himself for a challenge or help others to prepare for a challenge. Feces (waste products) float whichever way the current flows and serve no purpose.

A male will never be a real man until he is a father to his children. Fathers provide for their children's daily needs, protect them from things that may do them harm (even things they may like), and prepare them for life outside the sanctuary that should be home.

There's always a talk show concerning "bad boys and the girls who love them." Some girl is telling horror stories about things her boyfriend has done, her mother, sisters, and aunts are onstage crying about it, and some pointy-headed pimp wanna-be is saying ignorant things to get the studio audience whipped into a frenzy. Everyone is onstage except the one person who should be: the girl's father. Females respect and are affected by sensitivity. Males respect force and the perception of power.

No boy is about to disrespect or abuse the daughter of a man who has met him and informed him that his child is precious to him and that he will not stand for her mistreatment. That man, that FATHER, should ask that boy, "Are you the type of person you would want your daughter to go out with?" He would wait for an answer and if it was no, that boy would be excused.

Love. The word is thrown around too much as a substitute for *like.* "I love this song." "I love Quarter Pounders with cheese." "I love the Oakland Raiders." In truth, I like the song and the Raiders. I enjoy the taste of a Quarter Pounder. You can enjoy something or someone without loving them, but you shouldn't love anything or anyone if you can't enjoy them also.

Can you love someone else if you don't love yourself first? Not if you want to be mentally healthy. Too many people confuse attention, lust, and money with love.

Love is like faith. Faith without works is dead (nothing).

Love does things. Love says you dine before I eat. Love says you rest before I sleep.

Love accepts a smile as payment in full for services rendered. Love says, "Be all you can be, even if you have to be it without me." Love says, "I can do all things (lose weight, stop smoking, stop drinking, etc.) through CHRIST who strengthens me." First Corinthians, Chapter 13, tells what love does—much better than I ever could.

Imagine moving into the only house you'll ever have. You can have any house that's available, but once you choose it, unless it becomes unsuitable for human existence, you're stuck with that one and that one alone. Now exchange *man* and *husband* for *house,* and you have the terms for which marriage was meant.

Naturally, under those terms you'd be a lot more discriminating about whom you would pick for a husband. You'd ask the questions most people are afraid to ask when it's time for commitment. Questions like: Do you plan to work? Do you plan to keep yourself in shape? How many children do you want and how do you see us taking care of them? Who does what in and around the house? Would I be willing to take care of you if the worst happens, like a car accident, and you become a quadriplegic?

Assume nothing. Question everything before you take one of the biggest steps in your life. Others haven't, being too afraid to ask for fear they would ruin a good thing. They find their good thing is ruined because they didn't ask. This is your life we're talking about.

Other than choosing a deity to follow, a place to live, and a career to pursue, the person you decide to spend the rest of your life with is the most important decision you'll ever make.

The man you marry should realize he can do whatever he wants before he commits himself to marriage, but upon that commitment what he wants is discarded in favor of what you and the children need.

The person you marry should be the best example of a mate you believe you'll ever find. These are things you should know BEFORE you get married, not while you're knee-deep in the excitement of getting married. I've seen folks spend $25,000 on a wedding and wind up with a marriage that wasn't worth a quarter.

No one ever told me those things.

Love,
Dad

God and Religion

Dear Rhonda,

It has just occurred to me we've never talked at any length about God. You attend Christian school and we take you to church regularly, but do you really know what's going on? For that matter, do any of us?

Let me tell you how I see it. Have I ever seen God? No, but I've seen what He has, can, and will do. Are we sure He's a He? Would I know Him if I saw Him? Probably not, and I believe He would prefer it that way. I mean, breaking things down to the least common denominator, if you don't know who God is but you know you could meet Him at any moment, you're almost forced to be civil. That would probably be where the encouragement to love one another would come from. In the Bible, there is a passage about being kind to strangers because they may be angels in disguise. Once again, we are encouraged to be cordial. Personally, I see no harm in that.

Some folks out there doubt the existence of God altogether. I mean, if He exists and He's so good, why would He allow decent people to get into bad accidents, die from heart attacks and disease, or just have a hard time, when the low-down folks who doubt His existence do what they want, when they want? Why, when we sit in church, and the preacher says, "Stand on your feet and thank God for waking you up this morning," but two minutes later he says, "Sister So-and-So died in her sleep and she's gone to be with the Lord in a better place"?

Confusing? It is to me too. I think it's about being thankful for whatever you have—you know, taking what God gives you and winning with that. It might work, because if we do that, we can provide an example for others, who may think they have less than we have, to take what they have and win with it. They'll provide an example, and so on, and so on.

Then we meet those who ask, "How do we know God gives us anything?" People talk about God making the trees and light and rocks and whatever. How do we know there's a God?

I know there's a God when I look at the sun shining through the leaves in the trees in the morning. I know there's a God when I see the invisible wind move visible objects from one place to another. I know there's a God when I get a rush of energy on a golden autumn afternoon.

How do these things happen? How are they made? When did they start? I don't know. The answers are bigger than I, and that's a very hard thing for a nonbeliever in God to accept—the fact that something is bigger than they. They have to know all the answers so they can scientifically explain away everything. They can't accept that they may never know.

Don't get me wrong: Science is necessary and aids us immensely in our existence. It makes life easier and answers important questions. But the same mind that allows us to accept the fact that we can produce fabrics that will keep us warm in winter and machines to keep us cool in summer should be able to understand there is a power that exceeds our understanding.

Why not a being, a God who can do all things we can't, comprehend what we never will, and, according to our particular beliefs, make our way easier if only we show faith?

Granted, if you had been born someplace else, you might have been a Hindu or a Muslim or a Hare Krishna. As it stands, you're a member of an African Methodist Episcopal Zionist Church. I still haven't had anyone explain to me the difference between your church and African Methodist Episcopals.

I'm a Baptist deacon who looks at the Presbyterians, looking at the Lutherans, looking at the United Methodists, trying to understand the Pentecostals, who may wonder about the Episcopalians, arguing with the Irish Catholics about whether or not they'll stop fighting with the Protestants, who may believe they're better than the Roman Catholics.

Who am I to talk? Look at the Baptists alone. I don't know the difference between Freewill Baptists, Missionary Baptists, and Southern Baptists—much less the difference between the Church of God in Christ and the Jehovah's Witnesses.

It all appears to be subject to your own interpretation. All the aforementioned branches have two things in common for sure. They believe in God and His Son, Jesus. After that, everybody seems to go their own separate way. All lay claim to serving the one true God—several of them! (That's a Mark Twain quote.)

Some people believe that if you don't pray, sing, shout, kneel, speak in tongues, offer tithes, or dress the same way they do, you're a candidate for Hell's fires.

Religion has been used to keep people enslaved, lift up lowly spirits, bring down bank accounts, suppress civil uprisings, shame governments into doing the right thing, and heal drug addicts. As with money or guns, the determination of whether or not it's bad depends on what you choose to use it for.

Believers meet regularly in a mosque or temple or church or cathedral or house to listen to their leader, pastor, minister, bishop, overseer, rabbi, priest, father, or brother give his or her interpretation of what God would have you know each week.

I'm sure you'll agree with me when I say church is an interesting place. Go to the right neighborhood and you'll find a church and a liquor store on every other corner. I've often wondered why, if they all believe in love and Christmas, they don't get together once a month, pool their resources, and force banks, insurance companies, and real estate agents to help them start businesses and build homes.

Isn't it amazing how the same people who bend over backward trying to be nice and warm and fuzzy in the church are the same ones who will cuss you out if you block them in the parking lot, because they have to hurry up and get on with the rest of their day?

You know I've always said church on Sunday was nothing but practice for the big game you play Monday through Saturday. In other words, jumping up and down and whooping and hollering, or rocking back and forth, or whispering "amen" in your most dignified voice, or singing hymns on Sunday is just a wasted effort if you are not showing that love, justice, patience, kindness, forgiveness, faith, and stewardship from Monday to Saturday.

Small wonder the late Lenny Bruce said, "Every day people are straying away from the church and going back to God."

You're old enough to know now that everything that says it's holy isn't necessarily, and the devil can quote Scripture as well as any pope. Like anything else life can show us, the real proof of one's substance lies in the acts he performs—in his actions, not in the lies he tells during a performance. You know what character is? *Character* is doing the right thing when nobody is looking. Allow your spiritual leader to be someone *with* character, not someone who *is* a character.

My suggestions regarding God are these: Read your Bible so you can learn more about God and know better whom you believe in. Get to know Him well enough to trust Him. This means not having a problem saying grace (giving thanks for the food) in McDonald's or questioning what you don't understand. Be a little kinder than you have to be, but don't be gullible. Be patient, but don't be a doormat. Be forgiving, while keeping in mind the guilty party might commit the same act again, and if you must, forgive them again, then put some distance between you two.

Look for the good in everything and the God will come out in you. Remember those people who want to tell you about God are relating what *they* see. They are not God. When was the last time you saw a temple erected to a mailman? A pastor's most important job is to bring the word from God. They bring the message. They carry the mail. They're human and they mess up just like everybody else. What I'm saying is, don't worship them. Worship God.

Karl Marx once said religion is the opiate of the masses. There will always be naysayers and nonbelievers. What is important is what you believe. I believed so much I asked the guardian angel who did such a great job looking out for me to leave me and watch over you. I can vouch for them, they did a great job.

Love,
Dad

Death

Dear Rhonda,

I was five years old the first time I ever encountered death. I was in the first grade at Matilda Minor Elementary School, and after watching select Easter eggs hatch into baby chicks, my teacher let me take one home for Easter break. For one reason or another, the baby chick died, and I remember asking Grandma Emma why. She gently said, "I don't know, but I do know two things: Everything will die someday, and if you're good, you go to heaven." I asked what heaven was. She said that's where all the good people who die go. For some reason, I didn't ask about heaven anymore. I just felt sad about the baby chick.

Two years later Aunt Doris's daughter, Yvette, died and I went to my first funeral. They said she was sick with sickle-cell anemia. She was my playmate as well as my cousin; we were both the same age. I still wonder to this day how much more fun we could have had if she had lived.

The dictionary calls death "the end of life: the

Dear Rhonda

LIFE LESSONS
FROM A FATHER
TO HIS DAUGHTER

Demitri Kornegay

total and permanent cessation of all the vital functions of an animal or plant." To me, death means finality. The last time was your last chance. The good-bye we played with was for real. The see-you-later that will never come.

Baptists say that when someone dies, if you're saved, you're not saying good-bye, just "see you later." That may be true, but nothing is quite like the sense of utter despair you feel when you realize you won't see that person again in this world. There would still be so much left to be said, so much yet to be accomplished.

I suppose that is why, realizing how quickly events can change, I cherish every moment we spend together either on the phone or in person. I know I could lose you in a second, in a twinkling of an eye. I know I'd gladly give my life for yours because you are a precious gift who has so much to offer the world and you deserve a chance to show the good you can do.

It's amazing how much we assume in our lives. Because we've known them for as long as we can remember, we expect our parents to always be there. The same goes for other relatives and friends. We may even try to imagine what it would be like if they were gone forever. No matter how much you imagine, it's always ten times worse when it's real. When his mother died, Pastor Weathers asked me if you ever get over your mother dying. I said no, you just learn to live with it.

How would you treat a dear friend or relative if you knew next week you would be attending their funeral? That's why what we say and do must be tempered with love, because we don't know when they will be gone. All I could think about when both your grandmother and your grandfather died was, Last week this time, they were here.

Before your grandfather died from injuries sustained in a car accident, he said, "See ya later, sport." He was going out the door on his way to work. It was a regular day with nothing out of the ordinary. I never saw him alive again.

Your grandmother had breast cancer that caused her health to slowly deteriorate. Here was the only woman who could beat me running, the woman who taught me how to read and act, the woman who made sure I never had a bad Christmas or birthday, now too weak to breathe.

I've seen death come both ways, fast and slow, and neither is better when it's someone you love. When they died, I felt like the world should stop turning, but it didn't. As much as we don't want it to, life goes on, the world keeps turning. That doesn't mean we shouldn't grieve. We should. We must. When someone tells you they're sorry about your loss, just say thank you and go on from there. While you may occasionally reminisce, you cannot spend the rest of your life looking back. Don't lose today living in the past. Sure, it was more comfortable and things appeared more secure, but you must move on. Honor the memory of those you hold dear by showing the present how the people in your past helped prepare you for the future.

What gets to me is how people complain about things that their lives would be devastated without. I've heard mothers complain about crying infants, never once realizing that if the child died tomorrow, next week they'd give anything to hear that child cry one more time. I know guys who couldn't stand it when their moms sent them on errands, who now would love to run to any store, anywhere, if it meant their deceased mother would be waiting for them back in the kitchen.

They'll spend the rest of their lives missing someone they took for granted while they were here. They miss them so much or life is so bad that they consider suicide. Everyone wonders at one time or another what life would be like if they weren't around. Don't dwell on that. There is a reason we are left behind. I believe it is because there are still tasks for us to accomplish, more people who need our encouragement. If I had thrown up my hands and decided not to live anymore, there would be no "Men Under Construction" program, you wouldn't have had me to protect and provide for you, and you wouldn't even be reading this letter.

Before your grandparents died, doing these things never entered my mind. When they died, I was filled with such despair that "what am I going to do now?" seemed to be the only thought in my mind. The last time I asked that question, the answer came: You're going to do what they raised you to do, live so the love, attention, and encouragement they gave you will not have been in vain. Somebody still loves you. Somebody has a word of encouragement for you. Somebody needs a word of encouragement from you. Don't give up. Remember, everything will be all right in the morning; maybe not tomorrow morning, but sooner or later, one morning will come, and everything will be all right.

If you truly believe you can do all things through Christ who strengthens you, then wait, I say, wait on the Lord and things will get better.

People complain, "I've got to do this, I've got to do that." I say, replace the "got" with "get" and it becomes, "I get to do this, I get to do that." That's what life is all about, not letting one chance to live it get away.

If you can do that, when it's time to die, you'll be willing to go to the next phase, whatever it is, knowing you didn't waste God's gift to you. Try to leave the place a little better than you found it.

What's the next phase? I cling to the belief that it's heaven, a place you go to in the blink of an eye, the taking of a breath. Heaven is where all your questions are answered and pancakes are served 24 hours a day.

It is farther than far, yet closer than right here. It is a place where you're allowed to witness the highlights and lowlights of your life and those times you thought nobody saw. While you watch, you're being constantly reminded you had a choice. After the review is over, they ask if you asked for forgiveness for what you did wrong and your answer is the determining factor in whether or not you'll stay.

You will make mistakes. Learn from them. Pick yourself up, dust yourself off, and go and try to do the right thing again and again and again.

Remember, you are the star of your life's story and the film is running. If you allow Jesus to be the director, it will be an award-winning production.

When I leave you, know these things: I tried my best to be the father you deserve, I want you to go on and live your dreams, I'll be spending half my time watching God unfold the mysteries of the universe and the other half reuniting with Grandma Emma, your grandfather, cousin Yvette, the baby chick, and others, and your Dad loved you.

Love,
Dad

The Tragedy
of September 11, 2001

Dear Rhonda,

Recent tragedies made it imperative that I write you this letter. Last Tuesday, people—regular, everyday working people—were killed. People die every day. What made this different was the fact that so many died at the same time, at the same place. The real reasons why are still a mystery. The only thing we know for sure is that someone's loved ones are gone because someone, in the name of his religion, didn't care how much sorrow his brothers and sisters in the human family had to suffer.

I might be naïve, but I'm still at a loss to understand how anything this monstrous could ever be done in the name of religion. Apparently, the terrorists' goal was to cause as much damage as humanly possible. I must confess it's hard to use the word *human* here because the words *human* and *damage* should never be in the same sentence.

You were not created to be in a world such as this, but here it is. If no one else does, I apologize for the inhumanity that exists, the poverty, disease, famine, political strife, bigotry, corruption, and hatred you nor any other child bargained for when you got here. I must apologize, because I am partly responsible for your being here. I must apologize, because although you see me do all I can to change it where I am, the world still exists. I apologize, because at your birth, when others saw a baby, I saw hope. In your eyes I saw and see what could be.

I believed then, and I still do now, that if I protected you from danger, provided you with an opportunity to learn about and see and know of cultures and beliefs that were different from your own, and prepared you to live legitimately without me someday, you could be a leader who would practice tolerance. Tolerance is no more than the recognition that other cultures and beliefs exist and respect for the people who have them.

You, and others like you, were brought here to bring sanity to the world. Many went through much for you to get here, but you know that. Just like more went through worse for me to stand where I do. You see, you are my offering to the world's question, "Who can make this better?" You will have opportunities to show your wisdom. You will be provided with chances to be selfish. You will be presented with choices that will serve as examples for others. You will be able to choose whether or not you will stand up for those who can't, or for those who remain seated and comfortable. You will be someone's role model.

How do I know all this? Because I was your grandmother's offering to God and the world that had seemingly gone mad. And now you are mine. When the time comes to speak up, you will, and your words will give many much to think about.

Every child is his or her parents' offering to God and answer to the world's problems. I, like many other Americans, took personally the destruction of the World Trade Center towers in New York. I took it personally because the taking of innocent human lives in the name of terrorism does no one honor and wins no one paradise. I took it personally because I had to look in their eyes and pray the answer was no when I asked my friends from New York if they had lost anyone at the Trade Center. I took it personally when I had to ask the same question of my friends here and at church about those folks in the Pentagon. I took it personally because, in my heart of hearts, I knew the people who fought the hijackers in the skies above Pennsylvania did the right thing, as so many others who know me (yourself included) know I would have done. I took it personally when a terrorist made my daughter cry because she didn't know what had happened to her stepmother, who works for the government. The world is not perfect, but you can make your part of it better.

In the meantime, as you are still learning about this world and the people in it, I would have you remember these things: Talk with God regularly. When you do choose to speak, make your words worth hearing. Envision life as a suspect and it will keep you from becoming a victim. Occupy your brain with the question of how to turn the impossible into reality. Consider both the messenger and the message. Remember that a smile offers encouragement and lowers the defenses. Speak the truth, but do not expect it in return. Listen to your guardian angel. Don't lean on anything or anybody you are not familiar with. Observe strange-acting people, animals, and things from a safe distance.

The people who died last Tuesday had no idea it would happen to them. I do not know what, if anything, they left their loved ones. We can only hope they made the most of the time they had. We can only comfort the mourners, encourage the rescuers, rebuild our cities and our self-confidence, and preserve the spirit that says, "Out of many, one."

We can only pray they learned to do as we have, to say, "I love you" instead of "good-bye."

Love,
Dad

One Final Letter

Dear Rhonda,

Let's make sure everything is perfectly clear. You are not going to senior high school to party, although you may attend a few parties. You are not going to senior high school to dance, although you may attend a few dances. Although we are contemplating making this move from private school to public school to enhance your social development, you are not going to senior high school to socialize.

The only reason we are considering moving you from the private school you presently attend to a public school with a more diverse population is to improve your societal survival skills. We believe you should have an opportunity to join a math or science club, or be on a class trip or yearbook committee. If we allow this transfer to take place, you must remember you are just passing through this school; you are not going to stay. You are not going to drop out, as some individuals you encounter will. You are not going there to hang out; some you meet there will be doing nothing but hanging out. You are not going to school to have sex, get pregnant, and have babies. You will meet some young ladies who will do all three. You are going to this (or any other school) to further your education. You will employ your study skills to learn all that you can so that in two short years the state of Maryland's Board of Education will be satisfied that you have met *all* their requirements for graduation so that you can move on to the next level: COLLEGE.

Like you would at any other school, you'll be there to observe and learn and to learn and observe. You will encounter people who have no plans for or clues about what they are going to do once their time is up and they are kicked out of school with a diploma. That's right, they won't study or anything, but they'll be pushed right along to make space for the next one who won't do anything. They'll go through the motions and won't apply themselves because their logic is "I don't have to study and I'll graduate anyway." That's a loser's viewpoint. Remember, losers spend their lives explaining to anyone who will listen why they failed, while winners make no apologies for winning and look for new areas to conquer. It's true they'll graduate, but to what? Only then, when they attempt to enter the job market, will they realize how much precious time they wasted. Education in this

country is basically free up to the twelfth grade. Anything after that you *have* to pay for. The person who
goes through the motions will not have developed any
study skills or work habits, and therefore will not be
prepared to go to the next level. They will be stuck
mentally where they are. (Those who do just enough
to get by invariably find themselves getting passed
by.) Imagine being stuck at Hillcrest Heights Elementary School, or National Christian Academy, or
Full Gospel African Methodist Episcopal Zionist
Christian Academy, or Crossland Senior High
School. You should *mentally* outgrow them all. Like
any muscle in your body, if you do not challenge your
brain to work more than it is used to, it will not improve or develop; it will implode and deteriorate.

The world, the schools, are full of people who are
choosing, by not making a choice at all, to allow their
minds to deteriorate. (Remember, nothing comes
easy.) They are that underbelly of society which says,
"I'm just trying to survive out here." This is the rally-
ing cry and creed of the present, former, or future
convict. Dogs, cats, snakes, birds, and other wildlife
survive. People live. They live by the choices they, or
whoever is in charge of them, make. Your actions in

attending this or any other school will, from now on, be something akin to going through a McDonald's drive-through. You are passing through only to pick up a few things you'll need for your development and education. You should check before you move on (and you will be moving on) to make sure you have everything you came for, because you will have already paid for it—in this instance, with your valuable time.

Your time is precious. Don't believe me? Go to a hospice and ask, "Who needs a little more time?" Go to the oncology lab in a hospital and ask the chemotherapy patients, "Who wants a little more time?" Go to death row and ask, "Who'd like a little more time?" Your time, at this stage of your life, is best spent learning not just enough to pass through but all that you can, so it will help you. You are to observe those persons whose backgrounds may be significantly different from your own. First, to acknowledge they exist, and second, to learn the best methods of coping with them.

You are not here just to survive; you are here to *thrive*. These things we contemplate are meant to enhance your survival or coping skills. You may make new friends. You will meet new people. But your focus is to remain the same: Learn, learn some more, and learn it so well you remain on the honor roll, so that you may proudly step up to the next level.

You are my most precious possession. God will let me have you for only a little while before you must go and exhibit to the world all the things your mother and I have exposed you to. That is what it means to be a parent. God entrusts two people with a child and who that child becomes is a direct result of the parents' interest or lack of interest, direction or lack of direction, concern or lack of concern, love or lack of affection. It is a task that is not to be taken lightly, because if you take it on, there will be heavy days ahead. Those days will be heavy no matter what age at which you choose to take them on, but it's a fact, the older you are and the more education you have when you take them on, the better off you'll be. I have often told you that you should never be part of an organization you are not proud of. If you are a member, what are you doing to make sure you stay proud of it? Your name is *Kornegay,* a name that has a history of a people who have moved from servitude to self-reliance, from self-doubt to self-determination. Some who have worn that name have worked hard and succeeded. Others who bore the name worked hard and, for a short period of time, failed. Even those who failed provided us with a blueprint of how not to do something, so we wouldn't fail too. We've learned lessons from their failures. Proof positive that, if allowed, even our mistakes can teach us.

After being provided with the absolute best both your parents have chosen to offer you, you now have your chance to add your chapter to the family's history of excellence. We are a hardworking, educated, God-fearing people who are going to succeed. You now have the opportunity to bring either greater pride and accolade or shame and disgrace to our organization, our family. Do not take this lightly. From now on, wherever you go you represent your parents, your aunts, your uncles, your cousins, and more important, your ancestors, those people who dared not dream they would have what you and I have come to expect.

Make them proud that they sacrificed for someone whose face they never got to see. Make your parents happy that the time and effort they chose to invest in you was not in vain. Make your own mark in the world so that whether you are working or playing or studying, when your time in whatever endeavor is through, the people who knew you can say, "That's Rhonda, and I'm glad we had her on our side." And if they didn't know you, they'll say, "Who was that girl?"

Respect and prove yourself. Say what you mean and mean what you say. Do these things so by the end of every day, you can look in the mirror and honestly say, "Lord, I did the best I could."

> Someone sacrificed a lifetime
> Someone died to get you here
> Someone put aside their own dreams
> Someone cast aside their fears
> Someone said for me to tell you
> That you've got a lot to do
> But they also said to tell you
> That God would see you through
> Someone said, "Now you're the leader!"
> And it's time to take your place
> Listen carefully to the speaker
> Here's how you win any race
> Call on your Faith and Intelligence
> Embrace the Peace knowing God brings
> But heed the call HE makes to the Believer
> When HE says, "Arise, it's time to do great
>   things!"

Love,
Dad

A Letter from Rhonda

Dear Dad,

A father is defined simply as "a male parent." But to me, a father is so much more. He's someone who gives you more than just half of your genes. He gives advice, promise, his time, and his heart. A father never wants you to be harmed but wants every lesson to be learned. He never takes his time with you for granted or lets a day go by without thinking about you.

A father is one who knows what's going to happen before it does and tries his hardest to make you believe it. He can tell great stories with a good moral at the end and share vivid memories of the college years. A father's job is so important and his love so essential that without that guidance and love, a soul can go astray. A father is a spiritual leader and an example of what's right and what's wrong. He won't just give up or let his descendants go blindly into anything—not if he can help it.

A father is the one who will buy you all the junk food you want and help you eat it. A father will fight anything or anyone on your behalf. He will never let you go down without a chance at success. A father will refuse to be a "deadbeat dad," whether he lives with you or not. A father will sometimes be unfair, just to show you how the world is. But he'll always make it clear that if you need a break from the world, he's there for you.

A father will take you to the most action-packed movies and will tell you to close your eyes during the "adult" parts (no matter how old you are). A father won't let an event go by without saying, "Congratulations," or buying you a card—or just letting you know how proud he is of you. A father will share everything with you, even if he thinks he won't get it back (especially his videotapes).

A father will tell all his friends about you and brag with the best of them (even if you're embarrassed). A father will never settle for less from you, because he knows when you're trying and when you're just getting by. A father will pray for you and sacrifice for your well-being, which will in turn raise even better parents who will also sacrifice so their kids can live better lives than they did. This may all seem like too much for one man to accomplish. It may seem impossible. I know that no one person is perfect. However, this can be done. My grandfather has done

94

it and my father is doing it now for me. And as soon as the rest of the fathers in the world live up to my father's standards, the world will be a much better place—for the old, the young, and the unborn.

Love,
Rhonda

A Letter from You

Perhaps you have a life lesson, experience, or special message that you want to share with someone in your life. Below is space for you to write your own letter.

Dear   ,

Love,

ABOUT THE AUTHOR

DEMITRI KORNEGAY is a lieutenant with the Montgomery County Police Department in Montgomery County, Maryland. An eighteen-year veteran of the department, his assignments have included undercover narcotics work with the Special Investigations Division, five years on the SWAT team, and two years in background investigations. In 1992, he developed an award-winning twelve-week Rites of Passage program for young men called "Men Under Construction." The program, which has been running for nine years, teaches table manners, public speaking, setting a personal budget, and choosing the "right" woman, to name just a few topics. A gifted motivational speaker, Kornegay is well known in the Washington, D.C., area for the frank messages he has delivered to high schoolers. A graduate of the University of Richmond, he is married to the former Angela Nichols of Baltimore, Maryland, and has one daughter, nineteen-year-old Rhonda Michelle Kornegay.

*To book Demitri Kornegay for a speaking engagement,
seminar, or workshop, contact*

Nero's Publishing Company
P.O. Box 4407
Upper Marlboro, Maryland 20775
Phone: (301) 322-5088
Website: www.demitrikornegay.com